Because of This

Lao Tzu's *Tao Te Ching*
How to Live, Love, and Lead

Jim Teeters

Because of This
Lao Tzu's *Tao Te Ching*
How to Live, Love, and Lead

©2018 by Jim Teeters

Barclay Press, Inc.
Newberg, Oregon
www.barclaypress.com

Printed in the United States of America

Cover art: Zoe Hickam

ISBN 978-1-59498-043-5

Special thanks go to the Striped Water Poets of Auburn, Washington, for critiquing my rephrasing of these poems. I especially want to thank Brendan McBreen for suggesting the title. Thanks to Ann MacKenzie, who encouraged me with her praise notes on her critique copies. My wife, Rebecca, is my most prized editor; she has a good eye for improving my writing. And finally, a special thank you to my publisher, Eric Muhr, for recognizing the value of this work.

Contents

7 | Introduction

11 | How to Live

41 | How to Love

71 | How to Lead

101 | About the Author

Introduction

Me and the *Tao Te Ching*

I first encountered the *Tao Te Ching* in the year 2000
while teaching English at Wuhan University in China.
A student gave me his old copy with Chinese language
notes in the margin. I don't read Chinese, so those notes
simply showed me how hard the reader worked to study
and comprehend the writings of Lao Tzu. But I was drawn
to Lao Tzu's poems because they paralleled the way I
experience Christian spirituality. He emphasizes kindness
and peacemaking, and this speaks to my Quaker identity
and faith experience.

Lao Tzu lived and wrote in China from 640 to 531 BC. Lao Tzu expressed his care for the world by focusing his writing on how to live one's life, how to love, and how to lead. His work taught that good leaders respect common people and lead through inspiration, not with violence.

The word Tao refers to "the way" or "path" and Te means "power." Ching is translated "instrument." So the *Tao Te Ching* teaches how to be an instrument guided by the power of the right way. Lao Tzu speaks of being under heaven or of being in harmony with heaven's way. This power is spiritual in nature. One must be open to the Spirit, moving and breathing in concert with it. In the Quaker tradition of the Way, we stay in touch with the Holy Spirit and move in submission to the Inner Light, the voice of Christ who speaks to my condition. I have been a leader and educator in the Friends (Quaker) church, and I've practiced what Quakers call "communion"—waiting in worship for the Holy Spirit to speak in us and through us. Discernment is subjective at best—as is any leading of the heart. But when one truly seeks wisdom to guide action, there is benefit.

My Approach

I spent time studying several translations of the *Tao Te Ching*. I studied each one of the eighty-one wisdom poems—reading them over and over. I tried to understand what each poem was saying, then what each of them meant, what each of the poems meant to me. Only then would I begin to write. After each draft, I shared with my poetry group, Striped Water Poets of Auburn, Washington, and they offered feedback, questions, and suggestions for strength and clarity.

The *Tao Te Ching* seems to fall into three distinct categories: how to live, how to love, and how to lead. I found that the eighty-one poems can be separated equally (twenty-seven each) into the three subject areas. Poems are listed in sequence and by number in the *Tao Te Ching*, so the numbering will not be sequential in my rendering since I have organized them by subject.

Now I invite you to peruse, ponder, and discover from this ancient Source, filtered through my Western mind and my Christian, Quaker heart. And I challenge you: keep your mind and heart open as you read and reflect.

Chapter One:

How to Live

The only thing that counts is faith
expressing itself through love.
Galatians 5:6

Lao Tzu teaches us to seek understanding in order to find joy. The poems in this section demonstrate how difficult that can be. We are drawn into the mystery of life—the very mystery of God. We look within for the wisdom that resides in our spiritual nature as a result of our having been created in God's image. We need this wisdom—the wisdom that only God can provide. Finding it, we learn to accept and even to appreciate that there is much about God we simply cannot know.

Seeking worldly goods and selfish ends leads us nowhere. Still we strive. We strive for success. We strive for satisfaction. We strive for peace. Letting go can free us to grow and prosper into the peace we seek. Trying to be good—striving that we might obtain a heavenly reward—is useless since we are already blessed by the Creator. In accepting God's blessings, then, we find life's blessings for others and a blessed life for ourselves.

Lao Tzu draws our attention to the created world to show us how to live. We are surrounded by wonder and by danger; both beauty and devastation. With God's help, we learn to be like nature—to be who we are created to be;

to move and to be still. We open our lives to the beauty of God's presence, pay attention to the breath of the Holy Spirit. We wait. And we learn. Spirituality is a flowing force that overflows the materialistic concerns of a material world. What will I eat? What will I wear? Where shall I rest? What should I do?

Stop and center your life in God. Accomplish much by doing little.

1

Don't try to name
the unnameable.
You'll miss it.

See the mother
of all life; go ahead
call her creation.

Cling to self and
see only what is visible to all.
Lose selfish desire and
see the invisible Creator.

Both the invisible and visible
form a unified whole,
an enigma.

If grasped,
it's the doorway
to true understanding.

4

Oh Spirit of all things:
you seem empty,
but you are a never-ending Source,
infinite Creator.

You soothe our edginess,
reveal the mysterious,
temper our shining pride—
even so you join our earthiness.

How deep You are:
fathomless,
appearing
before all else.

6

The Spirit lives on:
mother of us all,
Creator, she is
unknowable,
flowing without end
within us.

9

When the cup is full
stop pouring.
When the knife is sharp
stop grinding.
A houseful of
silver and gold
will not make you more secure.
Self-satisfaction in money
signals impropriety.

To know when to stop
is a Spirit-born gift.

11

The spokes of a wheel add strength,
but the hole in the hub completes it.

A clay pot is lovely to look at,
but the emptiness within makes it useful.
Walls, floor, and ceiling form a room
but the space inside is where we live.

The material offers some comfort,
but Spirit brings true fulfillment.

12

Focus too much on
sights, sounds, flavors
of this world, and
you'll lose
true seeing,
hearing,
tasting.

Wisdom seeks the inner Source
not outer stimulation.

14

The Spirit of Life is
unseen,
unheard,
untouchable.

What a mystery we face.
We cannot grasp that
eternal,
unfathomable
Source.

Yet if we become
quiet,
humble,
fully present,
we will
Know.

20

Contrast yes and no,
good and evil.

This one wants fun,
a special day.
This one is removed
from both worry and pleasure.
This one doesn't smile.
Alone, he looks like a fool

Others busy themselves,
seek great discoveries,
consider themselves
wise, purposeful, in control.

The one who sees clearly
is nourished by the milk
of the Great Spirit Mother.
Ridiculous, some say,
yet this one drifts freely
in the Spirit's holy stream.

21

The all-powerful
Source of the universe
is unseen.

Signs and forms are visible,
never the Source itself.
Yet somehow we know
as through a glass darkly,
the origin of reality.

How can we know?
We must search
the Source
within.

23

Be like nature:
be natural—be who you are;
be still.
The wind blows,
passes away;
the rain comes
and goes.
This is the nature of
Heaven and Earth—so how can
mere humans create anything
enduring?

Wonder and danger exist,
a reality—if fully accepted,
we can live fully.

Only if we become one
with Heaven and Earth
can we find our
true being.

26

If we are self-centered,
shallow-minded,
this shows we are unrooted,
neither master of
self or others.

Rooted in true Source
we can dance, sing,
sway in newfound
serenity.

Overcome
the anxieties of
our troubled world,
cling to the true
Source.

33

To understand others shows discernment;
To understand self shows deepest knowing.
To subdue others takes physical force;
To subdue self takes spiritual fortitude.

Satisfaction is true wealth.
Moving with resolve is virtue.
Martial your resolve, stay centered.
You will die, but your soul is eternal.

40

Always start
at the beginning,
let go of pride.

All things arise
from Spirit.
Out of nothing
can come something
wonderful.

41

The Spirit of Heaven
is a mirror
into reality.
The wise one is brave enough
to take a long look.
Others are afraid,
just give it a sideways glance.
A fool laughs—
discounts it altogether—
and thus proves its veracity.

Truth can appear meaningless,
the way forward can seem backward,
great power can seem like weakness,
the Source of life can seem inadequate,
wisdom can seem childish.

To face the Spirit of Heaven
and look deeply within
reveals that
weakness is strength,
silence speaks truth,
wisdom seems incomprehensible,
yet all beauty and joy
are found there.

43

The spiritual
overcomes the material.
The Spirit flows
anywhere it wants.

So I'll let go,
teach with my mouth shut.
Do much by
doing little.

44

When you seek
external approval
or garner riches,
you fail to
find fulfillment.

Just be who you are.
Seeking prestige
or wealth
will leave you wanting.

Be grateful;
be satisfied.
All creation
will bless you

45

Trying to be perfect
wastes energy.
Be Spirit-filled.
Be yourself only.

From outside
you might appear lost,
faltering, ineloquent,
but within
you are on solid ground.

Peace and serenity
are your reward.

47

Wisdom can be found
within.
No need to go wandering.
View heaven from
your arm chair.

The more you focus outward,
the less you'll know.

Perfection is attained
with stillness
of heart.

50

To master life and death,
put your life in Spirit's hands.
Live moment to moment,
not clinging
but letting go.
Let your actions flow
from your inner soul's rhythm.
Live fully.
Anxiety can't hamper you.
Anger can't entangle you.
Fear can't disable you.
You'll be ready to live
and to die, as
death will come like rest
at the end of a busy day.

53

The Way of the Spirit
is free.
Those who take it
find a smooth road,
a highway of the soul.

Many people take
rough back roads—
so many distractions:
riches to seek,
fine clothes to wear,
tasty food, fine wine,
wars to wage.
They are blind
to the suffering, poor, and hurting.
It's the rough road of the robber.

The Way of the Spirit
takes no effort at all.
It is the Way of freedom.

63

Be more by doing less.
Accomplish more by taking a rest.
Taste more by eating slow.
What seems unlikely
may bring the greatest reward,
as when we treat our adversary
with kindness.

Big weeds grow from a tiny seed.
Infection comes from a small scratch.
Small acts deter disaster.
Humble beginnings can grow into greatness.

The wise one perceives potential
for great promise or pain
and acts early to bring the best result.

64

Stop, look inward.
Be aware by becoming still.
Notice your thoughts.
They are seeds.
Plant with care.

This may be difficult
because we want to
progress quickly,
but even the longest journey
starts with
a single movement.
A tower rises from
a single brick.

Just be.
Don't worry about failure or success.
Breathe.
Step by step,
life emerges.

70

The true way is seldom found.
Although the sages' words
are filled with meaning—
their actions well-reasoned—
rarely are they understood.

The answer
cannot be grasped
with the mind.

It is found in
the heart,
hidden by coarse cloth.

71

To know
you don't know
is a gift.
To think you know
when you don't
is a disease.

To know you are diseased
is a gift
that allows you
to lift yourself
into health.

74

Trying to hold onto
things as they are
is useless—things change.
Death comes to us all;
best not to fear it.
Knowing this, you can
accomplish much.

Trying to stop change
is like trying to
stop a train.
You are bound to
get injured.

77

Spirit teaches
balanced economy
like the tension on a bow—
top pulled down,
bottom pulled up.

This is not the way
of the world.
The richest want more,
take from the poor.
The Way of Spirit
brings the rich down,
raises the poor up.

The Spirit-filled one
gives from
an abundant heart.

81

True words aren't flowery;
flowery words aren't true.
The saintly aren't persuaders;
persuaders aren't saintly.
Wisdom isn't found
in outward study
but Inner Light.

Spirit-filled ones
are rivers of blessing.
The more they bless,
the more they flow.

The Spirit gives
without controlling,
and we freely ride
this river
of blessing.

Chapter Two:

How to Love

Love is patient, love is kind.
It does not envy, it does not boast, it is not proud.
It does not dishonor others, it is not self-seeking,
it is not easily angered, it keeps no record of wrongs.
Love does not delight in evil but rejoices with the truth.
It always protects,
always trusts,
always hopes,
always perseveres.
Love never fails.

1 Corinthians 13:4-8a

Lao Tzu wrote from a time and culture in which the decline of a dynasty resulted in militarized chaos as several noble families moved to consolidate their power. Yet Lao Tzu's sensitivity led him to write powerfully about the need for love and how to express this love. He advocated an emptying of ourselves, becoming free like flowing water. Water is soft and yielding, yet it wears away mighty cliffs. Water also refreshes. We must be like clear cleansing pools, letting our lives flow with love!

We learn that listening is loving—not by asserting our own way but by opening our hearts to the Inner Light in order to learn what it means to live with compassion and creativity. As a psychotherapist I learned that to be effective I must empathize, genuinely share myself, and show warmth in a non-possessive way. In fact, these qualities proved necessary—above and beyond my formal training—to ensure a patient's healing. I find these same qualities expressed in Lao Tzu's poems from thousands of years ago. The poems in this section help us to move toward loving more effectively.

Balance in one's life is also needed to love. One can be strong and assertive in compassion, but also gentle and nurturing. We are taught not to be a glittering gem but a simple stone. We need to stay centered and still as we seek the Spirit of Love within. It is in the still waiting and earnest seeking after the Spirit that allows our hearts to be changed such that we might find in ourselves the capacity to love even our enemies.

We are taught to be pliant and flexible. Being demanding and rigid-minded pulls us downward, making us captives of fear—especially when things don't go our way. The problem is trying or striving under our own power. After all, trying to be good leads us into morality (not genuine goodness), and morality leads to rules and rituals, pulling us further from our loving God. The Spirit of Love is present in us and with us. Rules can only control. Love, which is far more powerful than any rule, gives us the inner freedom to love both saints and sinners.

Finally, we learn that we reap what we sow. Sowing love for example results in joy, kindness, hope, and peace. When we live self-centered or rule-based lives, however, we turn toward warring and wanting more, whereas gratitude raises us toward heaven's door.

2

What we think is lovely
shapes what we think
is not.
What we think is good
defines the bad.

Life defines death.
Long defines short.
High can't exist without low.

The Spirit-filled teacher
sees clearly,
is not trapped
in the pull of opposites.
She teaches
with her mouth shut,
nurtures others
with non-possessive warmth,
setting them free.
Accomplishes
yet needs no affirmation.
Strives not
and
possesses all.

5

Life breathes,
is ever changing.
When we get stuck
in our prejudices,
we miss truth and beauty.
Best to empty yourself—
seek silence and balance.

Our world serves up
both wonder and danger.
The Spirit-filled one
judges not,
offers love to both
saints and sinners alike.

7

The Spirit of Love
is everlasting;
The universe
expands endlessly
because both are not
self-seeking but exist
to nurture.

The Spirit-led one
has complete fulfillment
through her
loving service.

8

Be water.
A stream flows forth,
refreshing all.
It doesn't struggle,
doesn't judge.

Make our world
livable and welcoming.
Be aware, generous, and honest,
fair and diligent,
blameless as a baby.

13

Compliments or insults
plague the soul—why?

Wanting compliments,
fearing insults—both
bind the heart.
If you are self-centered,
either overpowers.

Get free—become
one with the Spirit.

When you abandon self,
you offer hope
to our world.

15

True seekers
throughout the ages
have tried to peek past
curtains of creation.

In doing so,
they are respectful, aware,
not disturbing anything—
in tune with the earth
and the Spirit of Love.

Living this way,
emptying themselves
for the benefit
of others,
they create a clear
cleansing pool.

16

Finding peace
demands losing selfishness,
no more striving.
Instead of struggling
for control,
get quiet; seek
the Eternal Light—
our Source.
All else is dust.

Fail to find this Source,
and you'll wander in
confusion.
You'll miss heaven.

Gentle compassion leads
to humility, to dignity.
Surrounded by the
Spirit of Love,
you will face life
and death victoriously.

18

When the Spirit of Love goes missing,
rules arise to control.
When outsmarting others prevails,
hypocrisy gets a foothold.
When virtue goes missing,
rituals are born.
When trouble comes,
so do extremists.

24

Try walking on your toes
and stumble.
Try giant steps
and tire quickly.
Show-offs shed no light.
The self-righteous will be shamed.
The self-centered accomplish nothing.

If you seek
the Inner Light,
you avoid those errors.
Your life will bless others.

25

What we seek
existed before
the universe.

Calm existence.
Inexhaustible Source.
True guide
for soul's journey.

We call her Mother,
unfathomable comforter.
We arise from and return
to Her.

27

Tying a knot without a rope;
a shut door with no lock—
the wise understand.

Those who seek the Inner Light
walk freely with no rules or rituals,
like a traveler who leaves no trace,
like a speaker who leaves us speechless.
This one loves unconditionally,
shows compassion to all,
is a beacon for the lost,
yet many will not seek the Inner Light.

Following the Light,
one discovers
the Source.
Loving
leads the way.

Not following, not loving,
leaves the wise shaking
their heads.

28

Comprehend grandiosity
as well as humility.
Know darkness
as well as Light.

Be present, aware.
Live simply,
wasting no words or actions.

Live a balanced life,
an example to all.
Be strong and assertive
yet also a gentle nurturer.

Be one who serves others
as well as the timeless,
powerful Spirit of Heaven.

35

Show love.
It is irresistible.
All who follow
will be safe,
glad to live in harmony.

The world's attractions
captivate us, but
the Spirit of Love—
it cannot be taught.
It is just Truth.
You can't see it or hear it,
but it is available
in endless supply.

38

True goodness arises from
the Spirit.
It is effortless, selfless,
benefits all.
But goodness for show
is destructive.

Many follow religion's rituals,
its rigid rules.
This is the way of death,
the descent into hell.

If we lose true Spirit,
we try to be good.
If we can't try to be good,
we resort to morality.
If morality fails,
we have rules and ritual,
death.

The Spirited-filled one
moves from Inner Light.
Pure, selfless love
emerges from
the depths of heaven.

39

If you are not centered,
if you are not humble,
all hell can break loose.
You join with the destroyers
of the world.
If you are centered,
who you are, who you really are,
unified in word and action—
you'll reflect
the Source of Creation.

If you are humble,
realizing your dependence
on the Spirit of Heaven,
neither prideful nor arrogant,
knowing you aren't in charge,
willing to take a back seat,
you reflect the Source of Creation.

The Spirit-filled one
is compassionate, humble,
led by the Inner Light.
You may want to be
a glittering gem,
but it's best to be
a simple stone, lying quietly
in the riverbed.

46

When we listen to the Voice within,
we bake bread, make love, and raise our families.
When we fail to listen to that Voice,
we turn toward warring and wanting—the way of fear.

Warring and wanting draw us near to hell's gate.
Dissatisfaction pushes us in.
Gratitude raises us toward heaven's door.
Thankfulness offers abundant life.

49

Don't be a rigid-minded
know-it-all.
Be open to all hearts and minds.

Be kind to the nice folks
and the nasty ones.
Be willing to offer
an ear to the
honest and the dishonest.
Listening and loving
bring harmony.

The rigid-minded
are captives to fear.
To listen and love
unbinds them.

51

Our life emerges
from Mysterious Source.
Alive, we
are nurtured by goodness.
When we join with this Way,
we nurture others.

We offer shelter
and protection
for the weak.
We offer support
without possessing.
We help
without controlling.
We give,
expecting nothing in return.

This is love—
virtue in action.

52

The Spirit is a wonderful Mother
to offer such a marvelous world.
If you know her,
you will know her children.
You can be her child!

Live a life of love and peace,
and you'll truly live.
Seek after riches and power,
you only find trouble.
Be humble, see clear,
be caring, know true power,
be still, let go,
be open to the Spirit.
You'll gain eternal blessing.

54

Be careful, you will reap what you sow.
Sow carefully.
Your decisions today
will reach through generations.

Sow love in your heart, reap virtue.
Sow love in your family, reap kindness.
Sow love in your community, reap joy.
Sow love in your country, reap hope.
Sow love in the world, reap peace.
It all starts with love.
Do you want a world of
virtue,
kindness,
joy,
hope and peace?

Sow love in your heart.
All good things start from within.

55

The one who follows
Inner Light
is soft and
childlike
yet strong and resilient,
in harmony.
This one's passion
extends to all
spheres of life.
While giving all,
stays refreshed.

This harmony comes
from within,
balances
between control
and letting go,
has an eternal quality,
brings enlightenment,
blessings,
true strength.
The opposite brings
misery,
hastens death.

61

A central truth
in the Kingdom—
the greatest is the one
who serves.

Like a sea,
the streams pour into it.
Its greatness
comes from its low position.

When we bow,
offer friendship,
nurture the little ones,
welcome the stranger—
when we serve others,
we become great
in the Kingdom.

67

Truth has no rival.
It appears foolish,
yet it is profound.
If this were not so,
it would be profane.

These three hold high:
kindness, restraint, humility.
Kindness begets bravery.
Restraint begets altruism.
Humility begets perfection.

These days people want
to be tough but not kind.
Big shots.
They devour life.
But true life is found in
kindness,
restraint,
humility.

69

A saying:
Best not to start a fight.
Better to keep open and ready to make peace.
Instead of moving with passion,
move with compassion.
Go forth
without moving an inch,
doing battle without weapons.

Overcoming another
creates an enemy
where none may exist.
You destroy yourself.
In a conflict,
the one who shows compassion
wins.

76

We are born soft and pliable.
We die rigid.
All things begin
fresh and tender
then fade and rot away.

Listen! Be pliant.
Be flexible.
The rigid ones
are death's friends.

Bow and bend; be humble.
Let the prideful
and hard-hearted
inhabit the grave.

78

Nothing is as soft
and yielding as water,
yet it wears away
mighty cliffs.

The lowly overcome
the mighty.
We all know humility
is the best choice,
but who chooses it?

The one who blesses the lowly
will be raised up.
The one who takes on
misfortunes of others
is greatest of all.

Truth is paradox.

79

Even after a painful attack,
you must still love your enemy.
How is this possible?

Those who follow the Spirit
find ways to forgive.
Kind ones seek peace.
The selfish seek victory.
Spirit enjoys harmony and love.
Let this guide your life.

Chapter Three:

How to Lead

*The greatest among you
will be your servant.
For those who exalt themselves
will be humbled, and
those who humble themselves
will be exalted.*
Matthew 23: 11-12

Lao Tzu knew how terrible leaders can be: controlling, violent, self-aggrandizing. But true leadership inspires rather than controls, empowers rather than berates, and serves instead of demanding servitude. Again, the secret is in seeking guidance from the Inner Light. This is the gift within all of us: partly the result of having been made by God in God's image; partly the result of the Spirit, living and active with and within us. Instead of glorying in power and influence, the true leader is Spirit-led and humble. These principles hold true for business leaders, elected officials, pastors, teachers, and parents.

When leaders try to control others by making and enforcing rules, would-be followers are prone to resentment and subversion. That's because trying to control others often results in resistance and loss of control. Instead of controlling, a good leader empowers by example and by trusting their people to solve the problems they've been given.

Humility is a key virtue for leaders. A good leader listens whereas "a fool can't stop talking." Good leaders encourage others to find their own way forward and appreciate it when they do.

> Look at the mighty ocean
> power comes from her low position
> rivers race to her.

With such a leader, people get excited and want to do their best. Spirit-led leaders inspire and empower people, and things get done. People feel a sense of accomplishment. (We did it!) That is the result of a true leader.

Lao Tzu is also clear about the importance of peace. He consistently speaks against violence and militarization. That kind of winning—through domination and destruction of our opponent—isn't good for anyone.

> after the battle is won
> we've only killed
> others like ourselves

This is why the greatest leader is a servant-leader. We are to be humble and service-oriented in our genuine desire to help others—our workers, our children, our citizens, or our congregants.

> If you want to shine
> dim your light

We must move with the Spirit of humility and of servanthood.

3

Issue no awards,
no one feels discounted.
Don't envy the rich,
no one will cheat or steal.
Stop parading seductive desirables;
let people find
true satisfaction.

The Spirit-filled leader
frees us from wanting;
helps us seek simplicity
instead of worldly pleasures;
causes know-it-alls
to question their beliefs.

Effortless being,
instead of striving,
frees us.

10

Are you able to
stay focused even
as the world distracts?
Can you be childlike,
supple and innocent?
Can you break free from
doubt and darkness?
Can you inspire without controlling,
as a mother,
offering balance and sustenance?
Can you live in truth
wherever you are?

Bring spiritual nourishment
as you offer yourself freely.
Act with humility, and
never seek power over others.
Live this way.
You make Heaven visible.

17

The most profound leader
leads imperceptibly,
without fanfare.
Then in order of worthiness:
the beloved leader who is praised,
the one people fear,
the tyrant.

When a leader has no faith in people,
people become faithless followers.

The best leader does not boast.
In fact, when things are accomplished,
people boast about what they accomplished,
working together.

19

Stop claiming saintliness and wisdom,
and things will go better for everyone.
Stop boasting of kindness and goodness,
and you'll discover authentic love.
If none sought power and wealth,
we would be free of greed and violence.

Instead:
drop pretense;
be simple,
single-minded
self.

22

If you want to shine,
dim your light.
If you want to get ahead,
fall back.
If you want it all,
give it all away.
If you want to live,
then die to yourself.

The wise one seeks the true Light
that shines from the center of Heaven.

Letting go of self,
one finds true being.
Letting go of self-righteousness,
one finds true rightness.
Letting go of justifications,
one is found just.

29

Do you want to control things?
Get ready to be disappointed.

Let the Master do the work.
Otherwise, you'll make a mess.

Some act aggressively, others weakly.
Some offer warmth, others cold.
Some try to help, others destroy.

The Master sees clearly,
acts accordingly,
never selfish or violent.

30

The leader who relies on Inner Light
need not resort to force.
Force creates resistance.
Aims aren't achieved.
Trying to control people,
fighting and fury
only bring destruction
and despair.

The wise leader
seeks peace, not strife;
trusts deepest knowing, not pride;
depends on inner truth, not outward approval.
Worldly power offers security,
but this wall collapses.

31

Weapons are disgusting.
The wise one
hates them.

Weapons serve evil,
the opposite of wisdom.
Gentleness and self-control
are best.
Don't be seduced by power,
war-glory;
those who revel in war
are killers at heart.
They will fail to find
peace of mind.

War is
a funeral.
After the battle's won,
we've only killed
others like ourselves.
And we mourn.

32

The eternal Spirit
is measureless—
unseen and unheard.

If leaders would
open their hearts to its
delicate truth,
heaven and earth would rejoice.
A fragrance of joy would
envelop their followers,
no orders needed because
the rules would be written
on their hearts.

When we attempt to measure,
make distinctions,
it seems to give us power.
When we name and classify,
the result can be disastrous.

Leaders, let go of distinctions.
Let the Spirit flow
like a river through
your heart.

34

The eternal Spirit
floods the universe.

It is the cause of existence.
Demands nothing,
offers life freely,
has no need.
It is available to all,
not as ruler,
yet holds all power.
It teaches us this:
become great
by being a servant.

36

To breathe in,
one must first breathe out.
To release pain,
one must first accept it.
To hold onto something,
one must first let it go.

An eternal truth:
soft and vulnerable overcome
rigid and proud.
A true leader's strength
is not clever words or actions
but deep, still waters
of the Spirit within.

37

When you follow Spirit,
things fall into place,
nothing is left undone.

If leaders could learn,
disharmony would dissolve,
people would be happy,
accomplish great things.
True simplicity would evolve.
People would get along,
their desires fulfilled.

Peace, finally!

42

One becomes two.
Two becomes three.
The Trinity creates all things
in a dance of
feminine and masculine,
perfect harmony.

Craving power
disrupts perfection.
If you try to gain,
you lose.
If you are willing to lose
for the benefit of all,
you will gain all.

If you hurt others,
your end will be a disaster.
This is certain.

48

Seek knowledge and increase.
Seek Spirit and let go.

By letting go of self,
self-fulfillment is possible.
Once fulfilled,
you can influence
without wanting to control.

56

The wise one
doesn't say much,
but when she does,
you want to hear.
The fool
can't stop talking.

The wise one
has a Spirit of calmness.
She
is not strident,
confounded nor prideful.
She is both radiant
and earthly.

Seek her Source to
love your enemies,
remain calm in crisis,
walk with humility.
This way you will
live honorably,
store up eternal
treasure.

57

Typically what you want is to
make rules for predictability and
fight unpredictability.

But listen to the Spirit.
The more rules you make, the more they are broken.
The more weapons you have, the darker the nation.
The more clever your plan, the weirder things get.
The harder you try, the more alienation develops.

Become tranquil; people become more productive.
Don't interfere; people prosper.
Be still and reflect; peacefulness results.
Don't try to get your own way; the Way will emerge.
Give up desire; find joy.

58

When a leader is humble,
the people are more trustworthy.
When a leader is controlling,
the people are anxious, contentious.

Without a sense of justice,
even good folk become deceitful,
start a downward spiral.

A Spirit-led leader
walks upright, not prideful;
demonstrates, doesn't lecture;
inspires forthrightness by example.
She seeks the Inner Light
and finds her own.

59

To be a leader who blesses our world,
don't seek power and control.
Instead, listen and respond.
Let selflessness be your guide.
Then you are ready for authority.

You will be a strong mother
to our land, offering
depth of knowing,
spiritual wisdom,
long-lasting worth.

60

Want to know how to lead a great nation?
It's like frying small fish
(carefully, gently, don't overdo it).

Lead by Spirit,
evil is kept at bay or
its effect mitigated.

The Spirit-led leader
heals, doesn't harm,
and virtue blossoms.

62

The Inner Light
cannot be earned.
It is a treasure
offered freely,
a gift of life
from the Creator.

This gift is a refuge
for the virtuous.
It offers forgiveness
to evil doers.

When someone is selected
for office,
we tend to offer
knowledge, skill,
assistance.
But the greatest gift
is Inner Light.

Those who seek it
find it.
Those who err
find forgiveness.

65

Good leaders
encourage people
to find their own way.
They lead simply and
by example,
not cleverness.

No need for grand edifices,
great centers of learning.
Instead, each one teaches one.

When leaders are
in touch with Inner Spirit,
harmony happens.
They show us that life
can be full of
love,
joy,
peace.

66

Look at the mighty ocean.
Power comes from her low position—
rivers race to her.

If you want to lead,
you must learn to be humble.
If you want to inspire,
listen to those you lead.
With such a leader,
people feel empowered.
When she speaks,
people get excited.

Everyone wants to follow her.
There is no contention.
She is beloved, completely in charge.

68

When a warrior seeks peace,
when a fighter embraces the opponent,
when a leader is a humble servant,

then true harmony has come,
then people are empowered.

Heaven's perfection has emerged.

72

Self-centered leaders
cause people to suffer.
When leaders get in the way,
nothing worthwhile gets done.

Bosses striving selfishly
defeat themselves.
Only by serving others
can their cause be served.

73

Some actions
lead to safety.
Others put us at risk.
We face both
danger and wonder.
This is how life is.

The Spirit-filled one
doesn't fight, yet wins;
says little, but shares much;
will show up at just the right time;
is at ease, yet gets the
job done.

The Spirit is unseen
yet no one escapes
her influence.

75

When leaders want control,
people grow angry and
little is accomplished.
Where there is little hope,
life has no joy; death wins.

Leaders who serve
bring hope.
Leaders who control
serve up death.

80

If governed well,
folks remain in a
place of peace.
No need
for diversion,
travel or war.
They are content to
enjoy each meal
and its artistry
with joy and prayer.
There may be
other ways or places
to live,
but it's
so serene
right here.

About the Author

Jim Teeters is a retired social worker, writer, and seminar leader. He holds a Master's Degree in Social Work from the University of Hawaii and a Writer's Certificate from the University of Washington Extension. Jim is the author of two "how to teach" books: *Teach with Style* (ASTD Press, 2013) and *Going Intergenerational* (Barclay Press, 2010). His poetry collections are as follows: *Being, Doing, Loving (2002), If I Should Wake before I Die (2006), Morning Wings (2008), Don't Turn Away (CreateSpace, 2011), Reservations (Finishing Line Press, 2012)* and *I Gazed at God and Laughed (ATA, 2014)*. His poems have appeared in *Hiram Poetry Review, Beginnings, Arnazella,* and *Poets at the Kent*

Canterbury Faire and three anthologies. He taught English through poetry in China and has published articles in the *China Daily News*. Jim facilitates poetry groups at the City of Kent Senior Center, a local woman's homeless shelter, and teaches poetry to children in various settings. Jim is active in the Northwest Yearly Meeting of Friends and writes for the *Fruit of the Vine* quarterly devotional. Jim lives in Kent, Washington, with his wife, Rebecca. They have four children and nine grandchildren.